PARADIDDLE**BOOTCAMP**
DRUMKITWORKOUT

The Quickest Way to Master Paradiddle Grooves on the Drum Set

JOHN**HOFF**

FUNDAMENTAL**CHANGES**

Paradiddle Bootcamp Drumkit Workout

The Quickest Way to Master Paradiddle Grooves on the Drum Set

ISBN: 978-1-78933-221-6

Published by **www.fundamental-changes.com**

www.fundamental-changes.com

Over 12,000 fans on Facebook: **FundamentalChangesInGuitar**

Instagram: **FundamentalChanges**

For over 350 Free Guitar Lessons with Videos Check Out

www.fundamental-changes.com

Cover Image Copyright: Shutterstock, Evannovostro

Contents

About the Author

John Hoff is a professional drummer and educator who has been honing his craft for over twenty-three years.

As an adult, he studied under the most recorded drummer of all time, Bernard Purdie (James Brown, Aretha Franklin, Hall and Oates). Considering himself a permanent student of the drums, John typically spends eight to ten hours a day behind a drum kit and offers drum lessons on his YouTube channel Drum LCK.

As an educator, John has taught High School Marching Band, thousands of drum lessons, and countless workshops. Many of his students have been accepted to prestigious collegiate music programs across the United States.

At the age of eighteen John joined the United States Air Force and served on Active Duty until the age of twenty-four. He was enlisted from 2005-2011, but while deployed, always remembered to pack his trusty drum pad and sticks and dedicated all his free time to gigging, studying and teaching.

In 2017 he co-wrote and tracked drums for the single *Can You Relate?* by The Great Enough. The single went on to earn over one million Spotify streams. As a performer he has shared massive stages, opening for industry leaders Imagine Dragons, Young the Giant, the Wallflowers, Mike Shinoda (Linkin Park), Matt and Kim and many others.

Introduction

Rudiments are the vocabulary of all drummers across the globe and building an in-depth knowledge of them helps you communicate freely, clearly, and expressively to your audience. The Paradiddle is one of the most important rudiments, because when used to build grooves with the left hand (snare), they naturally create unique sounding ghosts notes that form perfect back-beat accents on beats two and four.

Most drummers are taught the single paradiddle early in their studies, but the vast majority never learn how to bring it to the kit. There are endless combinations available that help turn all the paradiddle rudiments into unique grooves. My *Paradiddle Boot Camp* has been created as a step-by-step system designed to help drum students master and *musically apply* single and inverted paradiddle grooves to create great-sounding music.

The idea came to me while I was serving in the USAF. I had completed a huge amount of training in my first few years, and I realized that almost everything had been taught through repetitive motions that combined slow and strict techniques. The goal was to develop muscle memory. It didn't take long for me to start applying this training concept to my practice routine.

Over the next few years, I developed my paradiddle groove system to focus on building and retaining muscle memory through repetitive motion, just as I learned in the military.

The key to programming muscle memory is consistent practice at slow tempos and every exercise in this book must be performed slowly to a metronome. Once everything feels smooth and comfortable, the tempo should be increased slightly by increments of five to ten beats per minute (bpm). A good starting tempo is 60 bpm, though you can certainly start slower depending on how familiar you are with your rudiments.

Good luck and always remember to have fun with it!

John

Get the Audio

The audio files for this book are available to download for free from **www.fundamental-changes.com.** The link is in the top right-hand corner. Simply select this book title from the drop-down menu and follow the instructions to get the audio.

We recommend that you download the files directly to your computer, not to your tablet, and extract them there before adding them to your media library. You can then put them on your tablet, iPod or burn them to CD. On the download page there is a help PDF and we also provide technical support via the contact form.

For over 350 Free Guitar Lessons with Videos Check out:

www.fundamental-changes.com

Over 12,000 fans on Facebook: **FundamentalChangesInGuitar**

Instagram: **FundamentalChanges**

Paradiddle Boot Camp Daily Objectives

The goal of practice for any instrument is to gain the freedom and independence needed to play whatever you want, whenever you want.

This challenge is all about mastering your ghost note placements and advanced hi-hat patterns, then applying them over popular bass drum grooves. It's about breaking free from the monotony of basic 1/8th note rock grooves and becoming more musical through the use of Single and Inverted Paradiddles.

Whether you want to use your lead hand on the cymbals to lock in with guitar and vocal melodies, or use ghost note patterns to lock in with the bass drum and bass guitar, you'll find yourself with countless new musical ways to spice up your grooves.

Completing this bootcamp will increase your independence and musicianship, as well as your overall freedom and control.

The following three time-based practice schedules have been designed to maximize programming your muscle memory through safe and practical means. The outline you use depends on how much time you have, but the 60 and 45-minute outlines have proven to be the most effective.

Three to five practice sessions a week is recommended for maximum progress, but that's certainly not mandatory. Even students who can only commit to one weekly practice session have shown great improvement over time.

It is important that you stick to the provided practice outlines to the minute. Just as in the military, it is crucial to stick to a strict, structured schedule every time you train.

Start slowly and take time to ensure your dynamics and technique are accurate.

60-Minute Practice Outline

The 60-minute outline provides the best opportunity for musical growth and retainability. *Do not* skip the warm-up and cool-down sections.

00-05 Warm-up and stretch

Start by slowly playing 1/8th notes on your snare or practice pad to loosen up. Next, gently stretch your wrists, forearms, and upper arms. End your warm-up with slow single and inverted paradiddles.

05-15 Perform ten Paradiddle Push Ups (see Example 1i)

Begin by playing your Paradiddle Push Ups on the snare drum or pad. If you are able to finish ten Paradiddle Push Ups before the ten-minute window is up, feel free to move onto the next instruction. If you are unable to finish all Ten Paradiddle Push Ups inside of the ten-minute window that's OK, just move on to the next practice instructions.

15-25 Review previous day's progress

A ten-minute review of your previous practice session will help sure up those newly learned grooves, and most importantly help warm-up your brain before you move on to learning new and more difficult examples.

25-55 Continue on to new examples

Use this thirty-minute window to focus on progressing through the book. It is important to play each example with the metronome at multiple tempos. Take your time and try not to move on until you are confident enough and ready to do so. Always remember to start slow and to stay focused on your technique.

55-60 Cool down

This quick five-minute cool-down is just as important as the warm-up. Cooling down after practice allows for gradual muscle recovery, heart rate and blood pressure recovery.

Muscle soreness and fatigue can be greatly reduced by following a strict warm-up and cool-down routine.

45-Minute Practice Outline

The 45-minute outline provides a great opportunity for musical growth and retainability. *Do not* skip the warm-up and cool-down sections.

00-05 **Warm-up and stretch**

Start by slowly playing 1/8th notes on the snare drum or pad to loosen up.

Gently stretch your wrists, forearms, and upper arms. End your warm-up with slow single and inverted paradiddles.

05-15 **Perform ten Paradiddle Push Ups** (see Example 1i)

Begin by playing ten Paradiddle Push Ups on the snare drum or pad. If you are able to finish ten Paradiddle Push Ups before the ten-minute window is up, feel free to move on to the next instruction.

If you are unable to finish all Ten Paradiddle Push Ups inside of the ten-minute window that's OK, just move on to the next practice instructions.

15-20 **Review previous day's progress**

A five-minute review of your previous practice session will help sure up those newly learned grooves, and most importantly help warm-up your brain before you start to learn new examples.

20-40 **Continue on to new examples**

Use this twenty-minute window to progress through the book. Play each example along with the metronome and at multiple tempos.

Take your time and only move on when you are confident enough and ready to do so. Start slowly and stay focused on your technique.

40-45 **Cool-down**

A five-minute cool-down is just as important as the warm-up. Cooling down after practice allows for gradual muscle, heart rate and blood pressure recovery.

30-Minute Practice Outline

This practice outline should be used for daily 30-minute training sessions and omits the material review section. Because of this, the 30-minute outline is not the best option in terms of retainability but will help you move forward toward your goals. It may take longer, but it will get the job done. Start slow and don't skip the warm-up or cool-down sections.

00-05 Warm-up and stretch

Start by slowly playing 1/8th notes on the snare drum or pad, just to loosen up.

Gently stretch your wrists, forearms, and upper arms. End your warm-up with slow single and inverted paradiddles.

05-15 Perform ten Paradiddle Push Ups (see Example 1i)

Begin by playing ten Paradiddle Push Ups on the snare drum or pad. If you are able to finish ten Paradiddle Push Ups before the ten-minute window is up, feel free to move on to the next instruction.

If you are unable to finish all Ten Paradiddle Push Ups inside the ten-minute window that's OK, just move on to the next practice instructions.

15-25 Continue on to new examples

Use this ten-minute window to progress through the book. It is important to play each example along with the metronome and at multiple tempos.

Take your time and don't move on until you are confident to do so.

25-30 Cool-down

This five-minute cool-down allows for gradual muscle, heart rate, and blood pressure recovery. Muscle soreness and fatigue can be greatly reduced by following a strict warm-up and cool-down routine.

Chapter One – Paradiddle Fundamentals

When learning any new skill, it's always best to start with the basics.

Chapter One is all about developing the necessary paradiddle fundamentals to complete this bootcamp. Every paradiddle rudiment can be broken down to a simple combination of single and double strokes. Pay close attention to the sticking of each exercise, as well as the placement of the accents.

Use a metronome and the charts provided to keep track of your progress. The purpose of this challenge is to build muscle memory, which needs to be programmed slowly and accurately before speeding up.

The key to attaining muscle memory is slow, smooth, repetitive practice.

Track Your Progress

Use this chart to track your progress of Chapter One. I've included a PDF copy of all these tables in the audio download files. You can get it from **www.fundamental-changes.com**

Beginner	Intermediate	Advanced	Warrior
60 bpm	80 bpm	100 bpm	120 bpm

Date/Example	Tempo	Date/Example	Tempo

Basic Paradiddle Rudiments

Each of the following examples should be practiced using the following routine:

1. Play each rudiment freely on a practice pad or snare drum until comfortable.

2. Add the metronome. A great place to start is 50 to 60 bpm.

3. Practice starting the exercise with the right hand.

4. Practice starting the exercise with the left hand

The single paradiddle is a four-note pattern that breaks down to a sticking of RLRR or LRLL.

In every exercise, focus on the accents placed on the first note of each paradiddle and make sure the non-accented notes, or *ghost notes,* are played with the stick starting approximately three to four inches from the surface of drum.

Example 1a: *The single paradiddle*

The inverted paradiddle is a four-note pattern that breaks down to a sticking of RLLR or LRRL.

Example 1b: *The inverted paradiddle*

The double paradiddle is a six-note pattern that adds two single stokes (RL) in front of the single paradiddle. It breaks down to a sticking of RLRLRR or LRLRLL.

Example 1c: *The double paradiddle*

The inverted double paradiddle is a six-note pattern that adds two single stokes (RL) in front of the inverted paradiddle. It breaks down to a sticking of RLRLLR or LRLRRL.

Example 1d: *The inverted double paradiddle*

R L R L L R L R L R R L   R L R L L R L R L R R L

The triple paradiddle is an eight-note pattern that adds four single stokes (RLRL) in front of the single paradiddle. It breaks down to a sticking of RLRLRLRR or LRLRLRLL.

Example 1e: *The triple paradiddle*

R L R L R L R R L R L R L R L L   R L R L R L R R L R L R L R L L

The inverted triple paradiddle is an eight-note pattern that adds four single stokes (RLRL) in front of the inverted paradiddle. It breaks down to a sticking of RLRLRLLR or LRLRLRRL.

Example 1f: *The inverted triple paradiddle*

R L R L R L L R L R L R L R R L   R L R L R L L R L R L R L R R L

Paradiddle Pyramids

These *paradiddle pyramids* were designed to help build the overall speed, articulation and control of the paradiddle rudiments. Each pyramid is created by combining all six of the previous paradiddle rudiments. The following examples should be used as daily warm-ups and exercises.

Each of the following examples should be practiced in this order:

1. Learn each example freely on a practice pad or snare drum until comfortable.

2. Add the metronome. A great place to start is 50 or 60 bpm.

3. Begin the exercise on the right hand.

4. Begin the exercise on the left hand.

5. When ready, repeat each exercise ten times without stopping.

The single paradiddle pyramid begins with four single paradiddles, four double paradiddles, then four triple paradiddles.

The triple paradiddles are considered the peak of the pyramid. The second half of the pyramid consists of four double paradiddles, then four single paradiddles.

The final measure is an accented single stroke roll. The goal is to flow through the entire exercise smoothly with precise accents and taps. Learning this slowly will help your progress tremendously.

Example 1g: *The single paradiddle pyramid*

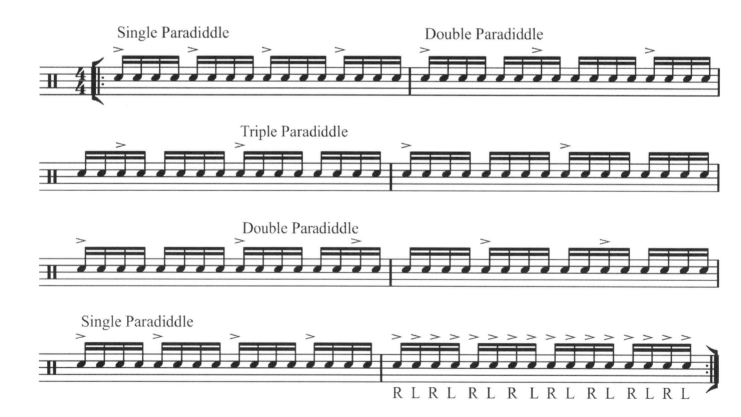

Just as before, the inverted paradiddle pyramid begins with four inverted paradiddles, four inverted double paradiddles, then four inverted triple paradiddles. The remainder of the exercise consists of four inverted double paradiddles, then four inverted paradiddles. The final measure is an accented single stroke roll. Again, the goal is to flow through the entire exercise smoothly with precise accents and taps.

Example 1h: *The inverted paradiddle pyramid*

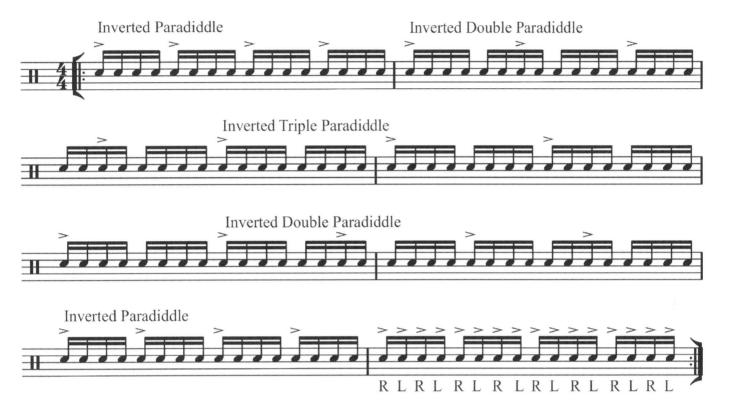

The Paradiddle Push-Up

The paradiddle push-up is a staple of the paradiddle boot camp challenge.

Military units all over the world have used the push-up as a motivational and strength building exercise for thousands of years. This challenge requires you to start each practice session with ten full paradiddle push-ups! It's important that you can perform at least one paradiddle push-up before advancing on to Chapter Two.

1. Start slow and gradually increase the tempo as the exercise becomes easier.

2. Use a metronome and keep track of your progress.

3. Perform ten full paradiddle push-ups without stopping

Example 1i: *The paradiddle push-up*

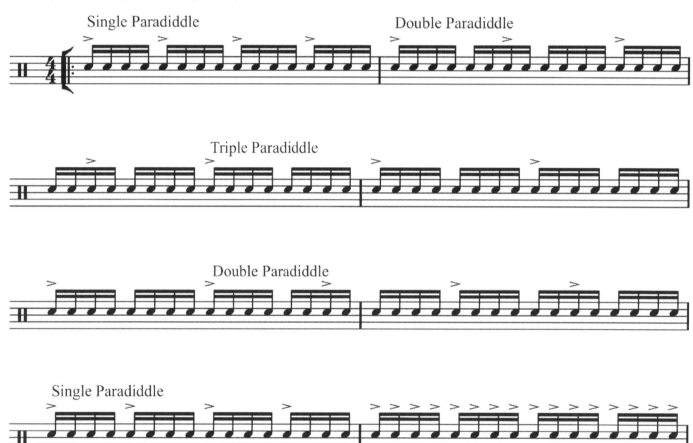

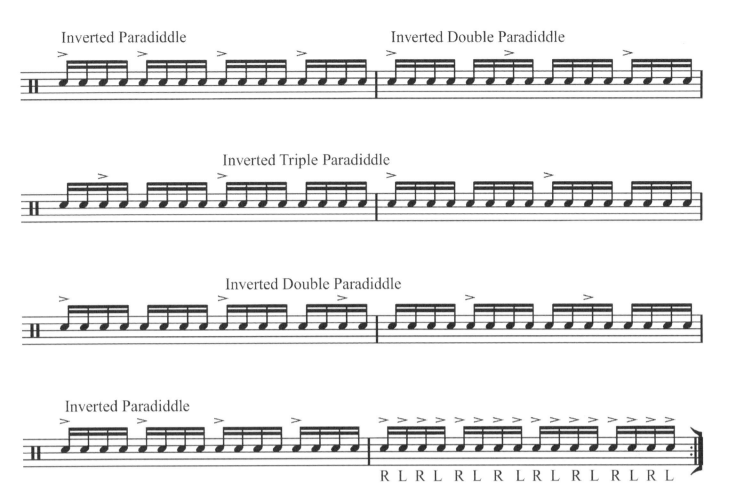

Chapter Two – Single Paradiddle Drum Beats

Now it's time to take the paradiddle to a new level. This chapter is all about applying the single paradiddle to the drum set as a groove.

Place the right hand on the hi-hat and the left hand on the snare. Do the opposite if you're left-handed. Pay close attention to the left hand. Make sure the ghost notes are significantly quieter than the accents.

We'll also add today's most popular kick patterns to the paradiddle.

The most important thing to remember is to play slow. Be sure to use your metronome and to keep track of your progress. Each exercise gets slightly more difficult as we progress!

Track Your Progress

Use the provided chart to track your progress of the Chapter Two.

Beginner	Intermediate	Advanced	Warrior
60 bpm	80 bpm	100 bpm	120 bpm

Date/Example	Tempo	Date/Example	Tempo

1/8th Note Bass Drum Patterns

The following examples apply different combinations of 1/8th note bass drum patterns to the single paradiddle. This means that each bass drum note will land on a downbeat or an upbeat. Stay focused on the placement of each bass drum and maintain strict paradiddle technique throughout the section.

The fundamentals learned in this section are extremely important and must be mastered before moving on.

Each example in this section should be practiced in this order:

1. Listen to the audio.

2. Begin the example slowly at your own pace.

3. Add the metronome to your practice. Start at 60 bpm.

4. Once you're feeling confident, gradually increase the tempo by increments of 5 to 10 bpm.

5. Play along with the audio track.

The following example places the bass drum on beats one and three and is often referred to as the *money beat* because it is the basis of most rock and funk drumming.

Example 2a:

Now let's introduce the world's most used bass drum pattern, *four-on-the-floor*. This pattern places the bass drum on all four 1/4 notes and keeps the groove driving forward.

Example 2b:

This next example pairs the bass drum with the right hand hi-hat by adding a bass drum to the "and" after beat three.

Example 2c:

The following example is similar to the previous groove. One bass drum note is added to the "and" after one.

Example 2d:

This example removes the bass from beat three to give the groove a fatter, more laid-back feel.

Example 2e:

Example 2f introduces bass drum to left hand ghost notes. Make sure to keep the ghost notes quiet. It can be difficult to maintain quiet ghost notes while simultaneously playing an accented bass drum. Take it slow and keep counting!

Example 2f:

This example adds the bass to the "and" after beat two.

Example 2g:

Now let's add a bass drum to each 1/8th note. Take it slow and focus on the overall sound quality of the groove. Make sure you have this example down before moving on to the next section.

Example 2h:

1/16th note Bass Drum Patterns

The following examples add different combinations of 1/16th note bass drum patterns to the single paradiddle. We'll explore placing the bass drum on each note of the single paradiddle, which will be more challenging than the previous section. For all of the ghost notes, ensure that your stick stays three to four inches off the snare throughout each example and maintain strict technique.

Each example in this section should be practiced in this order:

1. Listen to the audio.

2. Begin the example slowly at your own pace.

3. Add the metronome to your practice. Start at 60 bpm.

4. Once you begin feeling confident, gradually increase the tempo by increments of 5-10 bpm.

5. Play along with the audio track.

The following examples introduce the bass drum to the "e" of the paradiddle (the second note). Each of these added bass drums patterns line up with the right hand hi-hat.

Example 2i:

Authors pick: This example is a very popular funk, pop and rock groove. This groove shines in all types of music.

Example 2j:

Here's our first instance of "front-loading" the groove. There are three bass drum notes placed within the first paradiddle, and they all land on the right hand. Take your time and stay focused on the right hand.

Example 2k:

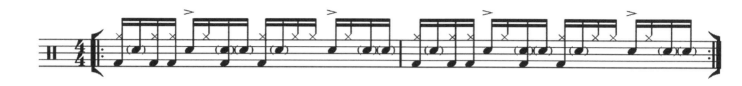

The next example builds on the foundation of the previous groove. The three-note bass drum pattern from the previous example is kept on beat one, but is also added to beat three.

Example 2l:

Let's explore more variations of the previous patterns. Focus on the bass drum notes on the "e" after beats two and four to give the groove a driving feel.

Example 2m:

Now beats one and three are identical. Beats two and four are also the same. Patterns like this can be used as a practice tool to develop your muscle memory.

Example 2n:

Fat-Back Grooves

The term *fat-back* originates from the Soul and Funk community of the 1960s to early 1970s. The term typically refers to a drum beat with accents on two and four and a laid-back bass drum groove.

The following examples introduce bass drum placements on the second note of the double left-hand notes. Take your time and focus on the transition between beats two and three. Also focus on keeping the double lefts quiet.

Each example in this section should be practiced in this order:

1. Listen to the audio.

2. Begin the example slowly at your own pace.

3. Add the metronome to your practice. Start at 60 bpm.

4. Once you begin feeling confident, gradually increase the tempo by increments of 5-10 bpm.

5. Play along with the audio track.

Authors pick: This example applies one of the most famous bass drum patterns of pop and rock music. Check out Walk This Way by Aerosmith for a popular example.

Example 2o:

Let's add two bass drum notes to the previous groove. The new bass drum notes are placed on the "and" after one, as well as the "e" after four.

Example 2p:

Example 2q adds a bass drum to the fourth note of the first and second paradiddle. This gives the groove a nice backbeat feel.

Example 2q:

This example adds a bass drum to the "ah" after beat four. Focus on the transition between each measure.

Example 2r:

Authors pick: The next example is an endless loop of the fat-back groove. This is a perfect exercise for daily practice.

Example 2s:

Here we add two bass drum notes immediately after the snare accent on beat four.

Example 2t:

Rock and Funk Grooves

In drumming, Rock and Funk are closely related. They share similar kick patterns and frequently use a backbeat feel. This section teaches you to add a few popular Rock and Funk bass drum patterns to the single paradiddle.

The following examples introduce bass drum patterns in groups of two that create an overall feel that's perfect for any rock and funk player. Remember to stay focused on your ghost notes and bass drum placement.

Each example in this section should be practiced in this order:

1. Listen to the audio.

2. Begin the example slowly at your own pace.

3. Add the metronome to your practice. Start at 60 bpm.

4. Once you begin feeling confident, gradually increase the tempo by increments of 5-10 bpm.

5. Play along with the audio track.

The next example adds two consecutive bass drum notes immediately after the snare accent on beats two and four.

Example 2u:

Example 2v adds a bass drum to the "ah" after one. This extra note front loads the groove and provides a very driving feel.

Example 2v:

This example places the majority of its bass drum notes on beats two and three.

Example 2w:

Example 2x alternates between two bass drum patterns. Beats one and three are the same, and beats two and four are the same.

Example 2x:

The next example introduces a new bass drum feel on beat three. Pay close attention to the alternating right and left hands during the new pattern.

Example 2y:

The following example combines multiple patterns learned earlier in this chapter. The pattern on beat three is the main focus of the next few examples, and will be used throughout this book.

Example 2z:

In the next example, the new kick pattern is added to beat one of each measure.

Example 2za:

Authors pick: This example combines all four of the major patterns learned in this chapter. Practicing this groove will help sharpen all of the sills learnt so far.

Example 2zb:

This pattern is a little more challenging. The bass drum patterns on beats two and three line up with the paradiddle in a difficult manner. Take it slow and count.

Example 2zc:

This example adds a bass drum on the "and" after one to the previous example.

Example 2zd:

This example introduces a new pattern. On the "and" and "ah" of beat two, the bass drum directly lines up with the double left. Focus on the volume and technique of the ghost notes.

Example 2ze:

The next example adds a bass drum on the "and" after one, as well as the "e" after four.

Example 2zf:

The following example is loaded with upbeat bass drum patterns. There is a bass drum on the "and" of each beat. This groove is a continuation of the previous example.

Example 2zg:

Authors pick: This groove builds on the previous example and adds a bass drum on the "e" and "ah" after beat three. This groove is an author's pick, because of how much fun it is play!

Example 2zh:

Authors pick: This groove builds on the previous example and adds a bass drum on the "and" after beat three and the "e" after beat four. It's great fun to play!

Example 2zi:

Authors pick: This example builds on the previous example and adds a bass drum on the "and" after four. This is the most fun example to play in this chapter.

Example 2zj:

Bass Drum Workout Grooves

This section adds multiple bass drum patterns in groups of four. These single paradiddle grooves should be used as practice tools to help increase the overall speed and articulation of the bass drum. Each one increases in difficulty as you progress.

Take it slow at first and be sure to use a metronome. The primary goal is to push yourself to new levels of speed and control.

Each example in this section should be practiced in this order:

1. Listen to the audio.

2. Begin the example slowly at your own pace.

3. Add the metronome to your practice. Start at 60 bpm.

4. Once you begin feeling confident, gradually increase the tempo by increments of 5-10 bpm.

5. Play along with the audio track.

In this example each note of the first paradiddle is paired with a four-note bass drum pattern.

Example 2zk:

The following example adds the previous four-note bass drum pattern to beat three.

Example 2zl:

In the final example of this chapter, the bass drum is paired with twelve of the available sixteen notes. This one is a workout and should only be used as such.

Example 2zm:

Chapter Three – Inverted Paradiddle Drum Beats

It's time to introduce my favorite pattern: the inverted paradiddle. This rudiment is a little more difficult to play than the standard single paradiddle, but the results are amazing. Place the right hand on the hi-hat and the left hand on the snare, or do the opposite if you're left-handed.

We'll also add today's most popular kick patterns to the inverted paradiddle. Each example grows in difficulty as you move through the chapter.

The most important thing to remember is to play slow. Use your metronome and keep track of your growth.

Remember that the key to attaining muscle memory is slow and smooth practice.

Track Your Progress

Use the provided chart to track your progress of Chapter Three.

Beginner	Intermediate	Advanced	Warrior
60 bpm	80 bpm	100 bpm	120 bpm

Date/Example	Tempo	Date/Example	Tempo

1/8th note Bass Drum Patterns

The following examples apply different combinations of 1/8th note bass drum patterns to the inverted paradiddle, which means that each bass drum note can land on a downbeat or an upbeat. Stay focused on the placement of each one and maintain strict paradiddle technique throughout.

The fundamentals learned in this section are extremely important and you need to get them down before moving on to the next section.

Each example in this section should be practiced in this order:

1. Listen to the audio.

2. Begin the example slowly at your own pace.

3. Add the metronome.

4. Once you begin feeling confident, gradually increase the tempo by increments of 5-10 bpm.

5. Play along with the audio track.

We'll begin by placing the *money beat* bass on beats one and three.

Example 3a:

Now let's add the four-on-the-floor pattern to the inverted paradiddle.

Example 3b:

Example 3c adds a bass drum to the "and" after beat three. Take your time and make sure the ghost notes are executed at the correct stick height (three to four inches).

Example 3c:

The next example is very similar to the previous groove. One bass drum note is added to the "and" after one.

Example 3d:

The following example removes one bass drum note and gives the groove a fatter and more laid-back feel. Stay focused on the left-hand ghost notes on the "ands" after beats one and three.

Example 3e:

This example adds a bass drum to the "and" after beat four. Make sure to keep the ghost notes quiet. It can be difficult to maintain quiet ghost notes while simultaneously playing an accented bass drum. Take it slow and count when needed.

Example 3f:

Example 3g adds one bass drum note to the "and" after two.

Example 3g:

The next example adds a bass drum on every 1/8th note. Take it slow and focus on the overall sound quality of the groove. Make sure to have this example down before moving on to the next section.

Example 3h:

1/16th note Bass Drum Patterns

The following examples apply diffcrent combinations of 1/16th note bass drum patterns to the inverted paradiddle. The bass drum explores every note of the inverted paradiddle and can be considerably more difficult using 1/8th notes.

Slow practice is a must. Stay focused on the placement of every accent and bass drum placement and maintain strict technique.

Each example in this section should be practiced in this order:

1. Listen to the audio.

2. Begin the example slowly at your own pace.

3. Add the metronome to your practice. Start at 60 bpm.

4. Once you begin feeling confident, gradually increase the tempo by increments of 5-10 bpm.

5. Play along with the audio track.

Example 3i introduces a bass drum note assigned to the "e" of the inverted paradiddle (the second inverted paradiddle). Each bass drum note in this example lines up with the right hand hi-hat.

Example 3i:

Authors pick: This well-rounded example works well in pop, funk, and rock situations. The inverted paradiddle hi-hat pattern sits perfectly in the groove.

Example 3j:

The following example front loads the inverted paradiddle groove. This example is considerably more difficult than the single paradiddle in Chapter Two. Take your time!

Example 3k:

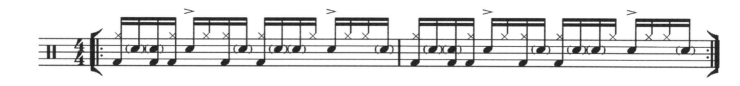

The next example builds on the foundation of the previous groove. The three-note bass drum pattern from before is kept on beat one, but is also added to beat three.

Example 3l:

This example explores more options of the previous patterns. Focus on the bass drum notes on the "e" after two and four. These bass drum patterns give the groove a driving feel.

Example 3m:

This groove is perfect for focusing on the timing and feel of the inverted paradiddle. The repeating bass drum pattern allows room to stay hyper-focused on the hands.

Example 3n:

Fat-Back Grooves

The following examples introduce bass drum placements on the second note of the double left-hand notes. Take your time and focus on the transition between beats two and three. Remember to keep the double lefts quiet.

Each example in this section should be practiced in this order:

1. Listen to the audio.

2. Begin the example slowly at your own pace.

3. Add the metronome to your practice. Start at 60 bpm.

4. Once you begin feeling confident, gradually increase the tempo by increments of 5-10 bpm.

5. Play along with the audio track.

The first example introduces a bass drum note on the "ah" after beat two. Beat three maintains bass drum notes on the downbeat and upbeat. This combination provides the foundation of this section. Take your time and focus on the transition between beats two and three. Remember to keep the ghost notes low.

Example 3o:

Now let's add two bass drum notes placed on the "and" after one, as well as the "e" after four.

Example 3p:

Example 3q adds one bass drum note to the "ah" of beat one (the first inverted paradiddle). This gives the groove a nice backbeat feel.

Example 3q:

The next groove adds a bass drum to the "ah" after beat four. Maintain focus through the transition between each measure.

Example 3r:

Authors pick: This example is an endless loop of the fat-back groove featured in this section. This is a perfect exercise for daily practice.

Example 3s:

The final example adds two bass drum notes immediately after the snare accent on beat four.

Example 3t:

Rock and Funk Grooves

The following examples introduce bass drum patterns in groups of two. These patterns provide an overall feel that is perfect for any rock and funk drummer. Stay focused on your ghost notes and bass drum placements. Practicing slow is the key to mastering these grooves.

Each example in this section should be practiced in this order:

1. Listen to the audio.

2. Begin the example slowly at your own pace.

3. Add the metronome to your practice. Start at 60 bpm.

4. Once you begin feeling confident, gradually increase the tempo by increments of 5-10 bpm.

5. Play along with the audio track.

Example 3u adds two consecutive bass drum notes to the "e" and "and" after beats two and four. They are played immediately after the snare accent on beats two and four.

Example 3u:

The following groove adds a bass drum to the "ah" after beat one. The extra bass drum note front loads the groove and creates a driving feel.

Example 3v:

The next example is a slight variation of the previous groove. It can be difficult to transition from beat two to three because it is a very busy bass drum pattern.

Example 3w:

The following groove alternates between two bass drum patterns. Beats one and three are the same. Beats two and four are also identical.

Example 3x:

This example introduces a new bass drum feel on beat three. Pay close attention to the alternating right and left hands during the new pattern.

Example 3y:

This groove adds a bass drum note to the "ah" after beat four. Each beat in this example is unique. This is a challenging example, so be sure to start slow with a metronome.

Example 3z:

In the next example, beats one and three are the same. This front-loaded bass drum pattern provides forward momentum and can be heard in hundreds of rock songs.

Example 3za:

Authors pick: This example combines all four of the major patterns learned in this chapter. Practicing this groove will help sharpen all of the sills learnt so far.

Example 3zb:

This groove is a little more challenging. The bass drum patterns of beats two and three are lined up with the paradiddle in a difficult manner. Take it slow.

Example 3zc:

The following example adds a bass drum note to the "and" after beat one to create a fat-back feel.

Example 3zd:

This example introduces a new feel. On beats two and four the bass drum is emphasized on the upbeat. The example features multiple bass drum notes combined with left-hand ghost notes.

Example 3ze:

The following groove adds a bass drum on the "ah" after beat three, as well as the "e" after beat four.

Example 3zf:

This continuation of the previous example is loaded with upbeat bass drum patterns with a bass drum on the "and" of each beat.

Example 3zg:

Authors pick: This groove builds on the previous example and adds a bass drum on the "e" and "ah" after beat three and is great fun to play.

Example 3zh:

Authors pick: The next example builds on the previous example and adds a bass drum on the "and" after three and the "e" after beat four. This is another author's pick because of how much fun this groove is to play.

Example 3zi:

This groove builds on the previous example and adds a bass drum on the "and" after four. All of the bass drum patterns (except beat one) in this example are placed in groups of two.

Example 3zj:

Bass Drum Workout Grooves

Let's now add multiple bass drum patterns in groups of four.

Each example increases in difficulty, and these inverted paradiddle grooves should be used as practice tools to help increase your bass drum speed and articulation.

The goal of this section is to push yourself to new levels of speed and control.

Each example in this section should be practiced in this order:

1. Listen to the audio.

2. Begin the example slowly at your own pace.

3. Add the metronome to your practice. Start at 60 bpm.

4. Once you begin feeling confident, gradually increase the tempo by increments of 5-10 bpm.

5. Play along with the audio track.

Let's begin with each note of the paradiddle on beat one, paired with a four-note bass drum pattern.

Example 3zk:

Now we can add another four-note bass drum pattern to beat three.

Example 3zl:

The final example of this chapter pairs the bass drum with twelve of the available sixteen notes. Try to practice this example for five minutes straight without stopping. Use the metronome to track your progress as you increase in speed.

Example 3zm:

Chapter Four – Two-Bar Phrases

Chapter Four combines everything you have learnt to this point. The primary objective is to create a repeating group of two measures known as a *two-bar phrase*.

Each example has two separate exercises. The first begins with a single paradiddle that moves to an inverted paradiddle. The second starts with an inverted paradiddle that moves to a single paradiddle. It's important to learn to mix and match these patterns to maximize the musical possibilities of paradiddle rudiments.

The goal is to learn to transition between the single and inverted paradiddles without altering the kick pattern. As always, pay close attention to the transition between the first and second measures.

The most important thing to remember is to play slowly and use your metronome to track your progress and stay in time.

Track Your Progress

Use the provided chart to track your progress of Chapter Four.

Beginner	Intermediate	Advanced	Warrior
60 bpm	80 bpm	100 bpm	120 bpm

Date/Example	Tempo	Date/Example	Tempo

1/8th note Bass Drum Patterns

The following examples apply different combinations of 1/8th note bass drum patterns to the two-bar phrase, meaning that each bass drum note will land on either a downbeat or an upbeat. Stay focused on the placement of each bass drum and maintain strict paradiddle technique throughout the section.

The fundamentals learned in this section are extremely important and provide a foundation for the work you'll do in the next section.

Each example in this section should be practiced in this order:

1. Listen to the audio.

2. Begin the example slowly at your own pace.

3. Add the metronome.

4. Once you begin feeling confident, gradually increase the tempo by increments of 5-10 bpm.

5. Play along with the audio track.

The following examples contain the *money beat* bass pattern. Pay close attention to the transition between each measure and remember to start slow. Focus on making the pattern created by the right hand on the hi-hat groove.

Example 4a1:

Example 4a2:

The next two examples revisit the four-on-the-floor pattern. This pattern places the bass drum on all four quarter notes and keeps the groove driving. Maintain strict focus on the transitions.

Example 4b1:

Example 4b2:

Examples 4c1 and 4c2 add one bass drum note to the "and" after beat three. Take your time and make sure the ghost notes are executed at the correct stick height (three to four inches).

Example 4c1:

Example 4c2:

The next two grooves are similar to the previous ones, but a bass drum note is added to the "and" after beat one.

Example 4d1:

Example 4d2:

The next two examples remove the bass drum note on beat three from the previous groove. The grooves become fatter and more laid-back. Stay focused on the left-hand ghost notes and the transition between measures.

Example 4e1:

Example 4e2:

These two grooves add a single drum note to the "and" after beat four. It can be difficult to maintain quiet ghost notes while simultaneously playing an accented bass drum, so focus on this and also your timing during the transitions.

Example 4f1:

Example 4f2:

The next examples add one bass drum note to the "and" after two.

Example 4g1:

Example 4g2:

Examples 4h1 and 4h2 place bass drum notes on each 1/8th note.

Example 4h1:

Example 4h2:

1/16th note Bass Drum Patterns

The following examples apply different combinations of 1/16th note bass drum patterns to the two-bar phrase. In this section the bass drum again explores every note of the paradiddle and inverted paradiddle. For all of the ghost notes, make sure the stick stays three to four inches off the snare throughout each example.

Slow practice is a must. Stay focused on the placement of every accent and bass drum placement. Maintain strict technique throughout the section.

Each example in this section should be practiced in this order:

1. Listen to the audio.

2. Begin the example slowly at your own pace.

3. Add the metronome to your practice. Start at 60 bpm.

4. Once you begin feeling confident, gradually increase the tempo by increments of 5-10 bpm.

5. Play along with the audio track.

The first examples introduce bass drum notes to the "e" of the paradiddle and inverted paradiddle (the second note).

Example 4i1:

Example 4i2:

Authors pick: As in the previous chapters, this well-rounded kick pattern works well in pop, funk and rock situations. The paradiddle and inverted paradiddle and a musical element to the groove.

Example 4j1:

Example 4j2:

The next two examples front load the paradiddle and inverted paradiddle groove. Pay close attention to beat one in each measure as the bass drum should sound exactly the same in both.

Example 4k1:

Example 4k2:

Both the following two examples build on the foundation of the previous grooves. The three-note bass drum pattern is kept on beat one, but also added to beat three.

Example 4l1:

Example 4l2:

The following two grooves explore more options. Focus on the bass drum notes on the "e" after two and four. These bass drum patterns give the groove a driving, forward momentum feel.

Example 4m1:

Example 4m2:

Authors Pick: This kick pattern was made popular by John Bonham on his recording of the Immigrant Song. The following example is a perfect groove to help focus on the timing and feel of the paradiddle and inverted paradiddle. This example provides a repeating bass drum pattern which allows room to hyper-focus on the hands. Take it slow and count when needed.

Example 4n1:

Example 4n2:

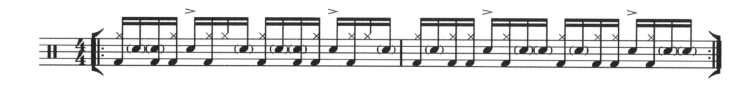

Fat-Back Grooves

The following examples introduce bass drum placements on the second note of the double left-hand notes. Take your time and focus on the transition between beats two and three. Remember to keep the double lefts quiet.

Each example in this section should be practiced in this order:

1. Listen to the audio.

2. Begin the example slowly at your own pace.

3. Add the metronome to your practice. Start at 60 bpm.

4. Once you begin feeling confident, gradually increase the tempo by increments of 5-10 bpm.

5. Play along with the audio track.

These examples introduce a bass drum note on the "ah" after beat two, while beat three maintains bass notes on the downbeat and upbeat. This combination provides the foundation of this section.

Example 4o1:

Example 4o2:

The following two examples add two bass drum notes to the previous example. The new notes are placed on the "and" after one and the "e" after four.

Example 4p1:

Example 4p2:

Each of the next two examples place one bass drum note on the fourth note of the first paradiddle and inverted paradiddle ("ah" after beat one). Another bass drum is placed on the "and" after four to give the groove a nice backbeat feel.

Example 4q1:

Example 4q2:

The next example adds a bass drum to the "ah" after beat four. Start slow and maintain focus during the transition between each measure.

Example 4r1:

Example 4r2:

Authors pick: This example is an endless loop of the fat-back groove. The transition between measures can be particularly tricky, so take it slow and count when needed. This is a perfect exercise to practice daily.

Example 4s1:

Example 4s2:

These examples add two bass drum notes immediately after the snare accent on beat four.

Example 4t1:

Example 4t2:

Rock and Funk Grooves

The following examples introduce bass drum patterns in groups of two that create a feel that is perfect for any rock and funk drummer. Remember to stay focused on your ghost notes and bass drum placements. Practicing slow is the key to mastering these grooves.

Each example in this section should be practiced in this order:

1. Listen to the audio.

2. Begin the example slowly at your own pace.

3. Add the metronome to your practice. Start at 60 bpm.

4. Once you begin feeling confident, gradually increase the tempo by increments of 5-10 bpm.

5. Play along with the audio track.

Examples 4u1 and 4u2 add two consecutive bass drum notes immediately after the snare accent on beats two and four.

Example 4u1:

Example 4u2:

The next two examples add one bass drum note to the "ah" after one. This extra note front loads the groove and provides a very driving feel.

Example 4v1:

Example 4v2:

The next two examples are a slight variation of the previous grooves. Pay close attention to beat three. It can be difficult to transition from beat two to three, because of the busy bass drum pattern. Start slow and count out loud when needed.

Example 4w1:

Example 4w2:

Examples 4x1 and 4x2 alternate between two popular bass drum patterns. Beats one and three are the same. Beats two and four are also identical. The two-bar phrase provides a unique hi-hat pattern which is highlighted by the bass drum pattern.

Example 4x1:

Example 4x2:

The next examples introduce a new bass drum feel on beat three. Pay close attention to the alternating right and left hands on "three" and the "e" after three.

Example 4y1:

Example 4y2:

The next two examples add one bass drum note to the "ah" after beat four. Each beat in this example is unique and creates a challenging groove that will push you.

Example 4z1:

Example 4z2:

In the coming examples, beats one and three are the same and contain a front-loaded bass drum pattern with a pushing feel. The transition between measures is the key component of this example.

Example 4za1:

Example 4za2:

Authors pick: These examples combine three of the major bass drum patterns learnt in this chapter. Practicing this groove will help sharpen all of the sills learnt so far.

Example 4zb1:

Example 4zb2:

Examples 4zc1 and 4zc2 are a little more challenging. The bass drum patterns belonging to beats two and three line up with both paradiddles in a difficult manner. Stay focused on the ghost notes in these areas. Take it slow and count out loud when needed.

Example 4zc1:

Example 4zc2:

The following examples add one bass drum note to the "and" after beat one. This gives the groove the nice fat-back feel we explored in the previous section.

Example 4zd1:

Example 4zd2:

The next two examples introduce a new feel. On beats two and four the bass drum is emphasized on the upbeat. A common mistake is rushing the "and-ah" of beat two.

Example 4ze1:

Example 4ze2:

The next grooves add bass drum notes on the "ah" after three, as well as the "e" after four.

Example 4zf1:

Example 4zf2:

The next two examples are a continuation of the previous groove. This groove is loaded with upbeat bass drum notes. Bass drum notes are placed on the "and" of each beat.

Example 4zg1:

Example 4zg2:

Authors pick: These next examples are two of the most fun grooves in this book. They build on the previous examples and add bass drum notes to the "e" and "ah" after beat three.

Example 4zh1:

Example 4zh2:

Authors pick: These grooves build on the previous examples and add bass notes to the "and" after beat three and the "e" after beat four.

Example 4zi1:

Example 4zi2:

The coming grooves build on the previous examples and add a bass drum note to the "and" after beat four. All of the bass drum patterns (except beat one) in this example are placed in groups of two.

Example 4zj1:

Example 4zj2:

Bass Drum Workout Grooves

The following section teaches you to apply multiple bass drum patterns in groups of four. The following single and inverted paradiddle grooves should be used as practice tools to help increase the overall speed and articulation of the bass drum. Each example increases in difficulty as the section moves along.

Take it slow at first and be sure to use a metronome. The primary goal of this section is to push yourself to new levels of speed and control.

Each example in this section should be practiced in this order:

1. Listen to the audio.

2. Begin the example slowly at your own pace.

3. Add the metronome to your practice. Start at 60 bpm.

4. Once you begin feeling confident, gradually increase the tempo by increments of 5-10 bpm.

5. Play along with the audio track.

In these next examples each note of the first paradiddle is paired with a four-note bass drum grouping.

Example 4zk1:

Example 4zk2:

The following two examples add the four-note bass drum pattern from the previous groove to beat three.

Example 4zl1:

Example 4zl2:

In the final two examples of this chapter, the bass drum is paired with twelve of the available sixteen notes. Try practicing these examples for five minutes straight without stopping. Use the metronome to help track your progress as you increase the tempo over time.

Example 4zm1:

Example 4zm2:

Conclusion

Congratulations on completing the *Paradiddle Boot Camp Challenge*!

Chapter One was all about developing the necessary skills needed to utilize the Single and Inverted Paradiddles on the drum set. Each example learned in Chapter One should continue to serve as your daily warm-up routine. Try pushing yourself to faster tempos while maintaining strict technique.

Chapters Two – Four taught you to add ghost notes and accents to your grooves through the use of Single and Inverted Paradiddles. You learnt each example as repeating one-bar and two-bar phrases. It is crucial for you to continually develop and finetune your paradiddle grooves.

If you have not already begun, take what you have learnt to this point and start exploring your own creativity. You should try writing your own bass drum patterns, add toms to the grooves, try moving the accents around and, most importantly, get out and play these grooves with other musicians.

Whatever you decide to do next, the most important thing is to just have fun with it.

John

What's Next?

If you are looking for more guidance on what to do next, below I have outlined a few concepts that will help. Each of the concepts should be applied to Chapter Two of this book.

Beginning with Example 2a, replace the paradiddle patterns with the new patterns provided below. The bass drum patterns must all remain as written. As always, the key is attaining muscle memory. Take it slow.

Double Beat Combinations

Double beat combinations can really spice up your grooves and stick control. With your right hand on the hi-hat and the left hand on the snare drum, try playing two single paradiddles and two inverted paradiddles inside of the same measure. It is important to remember to place a strong accent on the backbeat (beats 2 and 4) and to execute every other note at lower stick heights (ghost notes). Focus on the fluidity and transitions between each single and inverted paradiddle.

The Double Beat Hand Patterns:

RLRR LRLL RLLR LRRL or RLLR LRRL RLRR LRLL

Single Beat Combinations

Single beat paradiddle combinations can be very challenging. The paradiddle patterns change so often (every downbeat) that a lot of students get caught off guard. It is best to start very slow with each single beat combination exercise you attempt.

You may even want to practice these patterns on a drum pad before you add the bass drum patterns, to ensure muscle memory is achieved. As with every example in this book, it is important to play a strong accent on the backbeat (beats 2 and 4) and to keep every other note at a lower stick height (ghost note).

Stay focused on your tempo control and dynamics throughout each groove.

The Single Beat Hand Patterns:

RLRR LRRL RLRR LRRL or RLLR LRLL RLLR LRLL

Split Your Hands Between Cymbals

This method should be used in correlation with each example in Chapter Four for maximum effectiveness.

One method commonly used by drummers of all styles is to split your hands between the cymbals and snare. The best way to get started with this method is to place your right hand on the ride cymbal and your left hand on the hi-hat. Next you need to add the backbeat. On beats 2 and 4 play a strong snare accent with your left hand. It is very important to get your left hand back up to the hi-hat immediately after the snare accent. While you play through each example, experiment with your stick placement on each cymbal. You can get a wide variety of sounds out of most cymbals and changing it up in the middle of a groove can be fun and exciting for you and the audience.

Make sure you start slow and count when needed.

Two More Paradiddle Inversions

For an advanced challenge go back to Chapter One and try replacing each single and inverted paradiddle with the new inversions.

Although single and inverted paradiddles are the most popular and commonly used paradiddle rudiments, there are actually two more paradiddle inversions available to drummers. These patterns can be a bit more challenging because of the placement of each double stroke. In each of these two patterns there will be a ghost note placed immediately before or after the accent, and this can make it increasingly difficult at higher tempos. It is extremely important to start slow, to ensure the development of muscle memory.

Replace every Single Paradiddle with:

RRLR LLRL RRLR LLRL

Replace every Inverted Paradiddle with:

RLRL LRLR RLRL LRLR

Remember to follow the same accent and ghost note dynamics mentioned throughout the book and to keep detailed track of your progress.

Author's Acknowledgements

Writing a book is not as easy as I imagined! There are a handful people that I need to thank for helping me get to this point. Without any of you this book would not exist.

Bernard Purdie – Bernard, you have played such an amazing and important part in my career. I constantly remember all of our lessons in that New Jersey basement and especially when you took me on the road with you. You have not only been an amazing mentor, but you have been an even better friend. I could not have written this book without you and your priceless advice. Thank you, Bernard, I love ya man!

Antonio (Tony) Perez – Tony, as my high school drum line instructor you taught me countless lessons. You truly taught me the importance of rudiments and how to use them. Most importantly, you taught me how to create a strict practice routine and the importance of self-discipline. I truly believe that your lessons helped shaped me as a man, not just a musician. Thanks Tony!

Joseph DeTato – Joe, as my high school band director you taught me so much. You really taught me the importance of dynamics and how to play with other musicians. Most importantly, you were always there for me. Whether I was having personal issues or a hard time with a particular piece of music, you always took time out of your day to help me out. I will never forget the impact you had on my life. Thank you!

Alysia Hoff – My beautiful wife. What can I say? You are everything to me and I could not have done this without your relentless support and love. I can't say it enough. Thank you and I love you!

Fundamental Changes – I'd like to thank Joseph and the entire publishing team at **www.fundamental-changes.com** This entire process was a pleasure, and you and the entire team showed me nothing but professionalism and friendliness. You guys were always there anytime I had any questions or needed help. Thanks team, you rock!